The Mighty Seed

Inspirational Poems for Everyone

Esther Schultz Connor

TRILOGY

Trilogy Christian Publishers
A Wholly Owned Subsidary of Trinity Broadcasting Network
2442 Michelle Drive
Tustin, CA 92780

For information, address Trilogy Christian Publishing
Rights Department, 2442 Michelle Drive, Tustin, Ca 92780.
Trilogy Christian Publishing/ TBN and colophon are trademarks of Trinity Broadcasting Network.

For information about special discounts for bulk purchases, please contact Trilogy Christian Publishing.

Manufactured in the United States of America

10 9 8 7 6 5 4 3 2 1

Library of Congress Cataloging-in-Publication Data is available.

ISBN 978-1-64773-360-5 (Print Book)
ISBN 978-1-64773-361-2 (ebook)

Contents

....

Part 1

Part 2

Part 1

A Million Ways

Our God, Supreme Creator of the universe
His power cannot be denied
He knows the end from the beginning
He knows just why you cried
He knows your pain and sorrow
He understands your grief
You feel your life is over
He has a million ways to bring relief

The great I am, He knows your anguish
The things that cause you such dismay
Your inner thoughts and motives
Like a mirror are on display
You try to hide and posture
Act like you have it all in control
While your inner being screams out
Silently, see my heart, my weary soul

Does God feel a mother's heartache?
Can He see a father's pain?
When their offspring leaves their nest home
Sometimes never to return again
Can He feel that baby's heart cry
When deliverance seems denied?
How can they understand it
How can we when babies die?

So many unanswered doubts and questions
Seems the world has lost its way
Darkness seems to grow unhindered
Where is the welcome light of day
That's when the trust in God delivers
Watch the shadows run and hide
As the Son of God arises
In splendor of a million rays of light

Beams across the weary heart, soul
Hope and faith diminished now stand
Nothing past present and future
Can defeat the children of the great I am
In a million ways, He shows us
He is with us all the way
The problems looming, seeming majestic,
Are only shadows that we face

Look up, down, and around you
We serve a God of love and grace
A million candles glowing brightly
Can banish darkness, the gloom erase
God the Father's loving light streams
Can cheer the heart, heal the wounded soul
Just trust His word, await the answer
A million ways to reach your goal

A New Song

Gracious Redeemer
Kind blessed Savior
Mercy and truth my only defense
Redeemed by His grace
When I looked on His face
His boundless love has truly no end

Heavenly Father
Precious gift-giver
Gave Jesus to die in my place
In heaven, no sin
Can there enter in
I'm delivered, set free by His grace

A new song I sing
Of glory and praise
With hands lifted high, I rejoice
To worship my King
I owe everything to Him
Forever, I'll raise my voice

A Second Childhood

The change in posture, mobility's decline
I saw the vacant look, the distant smile
Come back to me, I'm here right now
No stranger visiting for just a while
We shared so many good times, laughter
Days of sorrow, toil, and care
Why have you left me now to wander
Far away to God knows where?

I saw the signs, more frequent mishaps
Right before my very eyes
I dismissed them, made excuses
It's only temporary, Satan's lies
Before I could grasp it, hold you forever
You seemed to vanish, quietly slipping away
I became to you a stranger
Seems like overnight our relationship changed

Science tries so hard to explain it
Such a crippling deadly disease, they say
Robbing us of precious time together
The quality of life changed to unease, delay
To combat this illness, research continues
A work in progress time will reveal
No cure yet, only trials, failures
God only knows how soon success will be

So I care for you, still very special
Love deserving though unaware
You have entered a second childhood
I am so glad that I can be here
Looking forward to times God promised
When all tears and cares are gone
And we walk in His divine eternal presence
Fully alive, completely knowing as we are known

A Symphony of Grace

His fingers touched mine
Blood dripped in between
Between myself and God
The covenant was sealed
Never to be broken
I'm His child divine
Signed, sealed, selected
In His image to shine

A dreamer He wanted
A family to share
All of His blessings
Both far and near
A world He created
A wonderful place
Then man He placed in it
A free will He gave

Satan, that deceiver
His doom he'd received
Was jealous of mankind
So made him believe
That God had withheld
What he himself had lost
To be as great as God
To know right from wrong

Man lost his innocence
His life was defiled
He wanted God's power
God wanted a child
Free will had a price
That man could not pay
God had a plan
That He put into play

A plan so magnificent
Only God could conceive
A free gift of righteousness
To all who believe
Satan couldn't imagine
The cross was God's way
To win back His children
It is finished meant grace

Grace that meant victory
A family redeemed
A new covenant holy
Deliverance revealed
God's children of freedom
Unfettered take their place
An army of believers
A symphony of grace

Abba's Here, Daddy's Here

Hush my little one, Daddy's here
Abba Father, it's you that cares
You hold me close
You soothe all my fears
Your strong arms protect me
All of my days

Daddy's here, Abba's here
I open my eyes to a big surprise
I lean my head on His breast, He cares
Daddy's here, Abba's here

You wipe away my tears
You banish all my fears
Abba's here, draw near
Daddy's here, draw near
He loves me
God loves me, He cares

All the Way

You've been a friend to me
A friend who always cared
Your kind compassion gentleness
You were with me all the way

You've never failed me yet
In sickness and despair
I called on you, a friend so true
You were with me all the way

All the way you lead me, Jesus
All the way never alone
All the way divine assurance
Let me know I'm in your fold

Precious Shepherd dear and gentle
Precious Savior, lead the way
All the way to heaven's portals
You'll be with me all the way

Although He Slays Me

Like a hummingbird's wings
In visions of gold
The Master Painter fashioned
Glorious to behold
Your presence was delightful
Inspired all that you did meet
Someone so special God gave us
Beautiful from your head to your feet

We thought the time we shared was endless
Freely given and received
To enjoy magical moments
Why would anyone believe?
That those moments, oh so precious
The countdown had already begun
The heavenly portals choir beckoned
Eternity's forever had tasted and won

The time was so short, only a little while
I was just beginning to know
The gift, the treasure God had given us
Why on earth did you have to go?
I so appreciate the pleasure
As you danced the songs of love
Now you're smiling with the angels
In your heavenly home above

Some people sit by the bedside
Of a loved one, fervently pray
For God to end their suffering, heal them
In some grand miraculous way
So much we don't know, cannot fathom
Many unanswered questions why
The tears are falling, hearts are wounded
We must trust Him while we cry

Some days are filled with pain and heartache
Immeasurable sorrow, death, and grief
Even a moment shared with loved ones
Can bring true pleasure, joy, and peace
Love has no boundaries, no distance
That time can conquer and divide
God pours out His love unmeasured
His divine will is undefiled

So say goodbye, my precious darling
Time moves on, its fleeting, soon passed
You brightened my days, my life's long journey
Your memory lingers, will forever last
The hope that God Himself has planted
In our hearts, brings us such peace
This is now, then is forever
Endless days that will never cease

So although He slays me, I will trust Him
To the end, He's in control
Every thought, His every motive
Is for our good to enrich our souls

Be at Peace

Be at peace, beloved children
Be at peace, open your eyes
God our Father never slumbers
Nothing takes Him by surprise
Knowing the end from the beginning
Means He remains in control
What Satan schemes and means for evil
God works all things out for our good

Be at peace, beloved children
You are precious in His eyes
Be at peace, you're not abandoned
Just hold on let faith arise
Be at peace, take each thought captive
Don't accept the devil's lies
Be at peace after the darkness
Comes the dawn, hope filled surprise

Be at peace, beloved, trust Him
He's a God who never fails
Giving us divine assurance
His kind comfort love prevails
All His promises, yea and amen
By His word, we will succeed
He is with us now forever
Rest in Him, trust, and believe

Be Thankful

Joyfulness gladness singing
For the abundance of all things
Be thankful, bless His name
He's every day the same
Joyfulness—be thankful
Gladness—be thankful
Singing—be thankful
Our God will never change
Be joyful, glad, and sing
Be thankful, bless His name

Let His joy be your strength
Be thankful, bless His name
Rejoice in Him, be glad
Sing praises He's the same
Yesterday, today, forever
Our God will never change
Be joyful, glad, and sing
Be thankful, bless His name

Joyfulness—be thankful
Gladness—be thankful
Singing—be thankful
Our God will never change
Be joyful, glad, and sing
Be thankful, bless His name

By Grace, We Are Saved

Jesus entered heaven's holy place
Into the presence of God
His blood brought redemption
And mercy to all
The ransom was paid
By grace, we are saved
Once sinners now children
On Abba, we call

By grace, we are saved
Given life, freedom anew
The spirit indwells us
His works, we must do
Share the good news of Salvation
Freely give as received
Redemption's a free gift
To all who believe

Soon the clouds will burst open
The trumpet will sound
Those who believed and received Him
In Him will be found
Changed in a moment to be like Him
Known just as He's known
Fully made perfect
En route to our new homes

We'll shout hallelujahs
A new song we'll sing
Praise, honor, and glory
To Jesus our King
Clothed in His righteousness
Like stars we will shine
Forever and forever
In His love divine

Come Dance with Me
(Zephaniah 3:17)

....

Dance and adore Him
Sway side to side
In sweet abandon
From left to right
Lift joyful your hands
Close your eyes, take a stand
Praise Him now and forever
Come dance with me

Dance and adore Him
Like David of old
He danced till he was naked
In the Bible, we're told
The trees and the Flowers
All sway wild and free
As the breeze softly whispers
Come dance with me

God the Father loves His children
Holds them close in His arms
Like a mother holds her baby
Keeps safe from all harm
Does He dance around the throne?
Rejoicing over them with song
Nature joins in with glee
Come dance with me

Dwell Safely and Forever
(Psalm 91)

Dwell safely and forever
In the Almighty's secret place
Underneath His shadow's border
In the multitude of grace
Accept now His sweet assurance
All who in His love abide
He will hasten to deliver
From disease's deadly tide

Dwell safely and forever
Snuggle 'neath His mighty wings
Underneath his feathers' cover
From the arrows' piercing stings
Nightly terrors, deadly mishaps
Thousands fall before your eyes
Angels gather all around you
Halt the enemy's dark tide

Dwell safely and forever
God has promised, gave His word
No evil comes against you
Demolished swiftly by angels' swords
Given charge, they stand all ready
To bear you up in mighty hands
Your footsteps will never falter
Strike no stone or sinking sand

Dwell safely and forever
No lion, adder, dragon fear
Since you set your love upon Him
When you call His name, He'll hear
He'll show you honor, His salvation
He will set you up on high
He will be with you in trouble
With long life, He'll satisfy

Fact, Not Feeling

I've been searching all my life
So many days of hurt and strife
Seeking the feeling, the joy, the delight
Trying to hold on to make it right
Feelings are fleeting, so soon they're passed
Striving to hold on to make it last
Am I to live a life filled with regret
To rue the day the times we met?
Each new attraction lasting just awhile
Beyond each echo each dream each smile

I must hold on to the things that are dear
Things that touch my heart unfilled with care
The rose's sweet smell, the lasting perfume
Raindrops that caress and dispel the gloom
The sun's golden warmth, the heat of the day
The moonbeam's cast shadows along the way
The star-filled sky speaks hushed glory divine
Saturating my soul, satisfying my mind
Speaking in hushed tones, gentle and sweet
Caressing my innermost rhythmic heartbeat

My heart held in hands, majestic and strong
I'm super-filled with power, the need to belong
In the cosmic pavilion to take my rightful place
To fully understand the meaning of grace

Creation's story of mankind's sad fate
The desire to manage our own lives filled with hate
When God the Father, all love, all holy design
Descended to hell to rescue His wayward child
To place him up high, honor, deliver him from shame
To live fulfilled lives, all glorious, bearing His name

Get Yourself Off Your Mind
(Reggae/Lively Beat)

Get yourself off your mind
Don't you take Jesus's place
He deserves all the praise
Give Him glory all day
When He hung on the cross
He had you on His mind
Don't be filled with your pride
Jesus loves all mankind

Get yourself off your mind
Wrap yourself in His love
He alone died for us
That's why He came from above
Bringing gifts for mankind
The sting of death did erase
"It is finished," He cried
Sent the downpour of grace

Get yourself off your mind
Give Him glory and praise
Get yourself off your mind
Thank God for mercy and grace

(Repeat last four lines)

God Cares

Uncertain times
Uncertain days
Uncertain moments
Uncertain ways
Our only hopes
In God alone
On Him depend
He cares for His own

When evening falls
Shadows appear
In life, in death
He loves, He cares
He gave His son
The world to save
When day is done
No victory the grave

God Desired You

God desired you
He called your name one day
He needs your special touch
And all you have to say
No one does it like you do
There's no one quite like you
The world it needed you
And God really loves your way

God desired you
The twinkle in your eye
That very special something
The hurt that makes you cry
The joy that you create
Whenever you are near
The world it still needs you
God made you that way

God desired you
Before your time began
He knew your special gift
The place you'd hold in man
In you, He placed the glue
That binds our hearts in love
The world it still needs you
God celebrates your day

God Knows Best

I would like to ask you a question
If you knew what lies ahead
If you knew the path your children
Would be taking, by whom lead
Would you have a sweet assurance
Or question every step they'd take?
Maybe even try to persuade them
To take another path that day

God in His blessed omniscience
Knows the path, the way we'll take
But He knows that worry kills us
We would be overwhelmed each day
We would celebrate the good times
We would leap and jump for joy
But how to celebrate if knowing
One of your dreams might be destroyed?

God, in His wisdom, does protect us
Asks gently, leave all in His hands
He knows the past, present, and future
The pressures we face, our lives' demands
Place the future in God's leading
Let Him have His full control
Let the past mistakes and failures
Be the past, not upset your goals

Daily bask in God's holy presence
Let Him lead your life each day
The future's bright, though path be narrow
Trust in God, let Him guide your way
God brings comfort, healing, victory
He's our hope, on Him depend
He's a God who is like a Shepherd
He's our God, our Savior, our Friend

God Offers Grace

Times are quickly, so quickly changing
Technology and new inventions prevail
But good old-fashioned values we learned
Should still be leading us along the way
The search for wealth itself isn't sinful
If it's kept in its rightful place
And the strong desire to succeed
Not a thing of shame or disgrace
Just remember unsaved loved ones
Need God's mercy and offer of grace
They are lost without a Savior
He must have His rightful place.

We have tasted of the good life
We have travelled far and wide
To drink so deeply of life's offerings
To enjoy all things that we desired
We found, at last, God's way's the best way
To reach out to Jesus and receive
The peace that passes understanding
When on Jesus we believed
The alternative was oh so hellish
Too horrible for anyone to take
Final separation from God and loved ones
When the God of love offers His grace.

God's Army of Believers

God's army of believers
Are conquerors by faith
The precious blood of Jesus
Won victory that day

Sin no more has dominion
For Jesus set us free
God's army of believers
We walk in victory

We're free to walk unfettered
We're free to testify
We're free to live for Jesus
In His image to shine

What joy His presence gives
What peace we can't describe
The knowledge that God's our father
That we have a home on high

As God's army of believers
We will take our rightful place
We will share and show to others
Gods free gift of Amazing Grace

God's Brilliant Plan

God created a world most beautiful
Gave man power to rule as King
All that mankind wanted or needed
He was given everything
God wanted no robotic gestures of love
He gave man the power to choose
To love completely his Creator God
To decide to win or lose
To be in charge of his own actions
To control his own destiny
To defy God and choose the Serpent
Or live in divine ecstasy
Free will had a horrid consequence
Mankind took the bait, blame his only defense
How could mankind refuse God's wonderful love
To give his power over to Satan?
To know evil and to know good
God, in His omniscience, had a plan
Unknown to Satan, unknown to man
From the beginning of time when it all began
Jesus would die for all mankind
To put sin to death, prove Satan a liar
To freely give righteousness if man desired
To those who chose to accept and receive
God's gift to mankind, and believe
Jesus died doing His Father's will
Choosing God's way as the best one still
Rose from the dead, went to heaven to prove
To love God with free will, is to win, not lose
To let God control one's destiny and life
Is to fulfill God's plan for man to be truly wise

God's Constant Care
(Psalm 139)

When your world's turned upside down
When things seem to be out of control
Remember to stand on God's words
For your life and safety, He has a goal

He'll be with you in the darkness
He will keep your pathway bright
He will hold you up, lest you fall
He'll be with you day and night

He'll surround you with His presence
He knows if you go out or stay in
Nothing is hidden from His eyes
You're His child, you belong to Him

He knew you before your day dawned
You are fearfully and wonderfully made
When evil conspires to overtake you
God your Father leads each step of the way

So look up instead, sing His praises
He inhabits and dwells in each song
God's constant care means your victory
So rejoice in Him all the day long

God's Plan

God had a plan
Unknown to man
Satan chuckled with glee
As Pilate washed his hands

Pawns in God's plan
The perfect design
Perfected and fashioned
To save all mankind

To those who believe
Put their trust in Him
The precious Savior's blood
Will save from all sin

The pawns came deceived
As Jesus did pray
The sweat dripped as blood
Became Satan's mistake

"Crucify Him," they cried
As the witnesses lied
No words did Jesus say
Crowned with thorns on that day

God's plan was real
Our Salvation was sealed
Jesus died rose again
God's plan was made plain

Grace Changes Me

Every moment of every day
I choose to live the Godly way
His grace was greater my sin destroyed
I live by the faith of the Son of God

Grace changes me His love divine
Has captured and changed this heart of mine
Delivered I stand a smile on my face
Redeemed by His blood a mouth full of praise

The difference, my friends, is so clear to see
His grace, so amazing, enraptures me
How can such love, such fellowship be
Extended to anyone who believes?

This grace extended so vast so free
Soothed my weary soul and rescued me
From the doubt-filled religion, the disbelief
To new life in Jesus where grace changes me

He Came to Die

Jesus was born to die
To die for your sins and mine
To give His sinless life
A sacrifice for all mankind

To lay His life down that day
When men screamed, "Crucify"
He lovingly spoke these words
"Father, forgive them," He cried

They had no idea the cost
Of Jesus Christ's holy blood
The Savior He took the blame
The matchless beloved Son of God

He came to die in disgrace
Took all of our sins placed upon Him
For our Salvation by God's grace
Mercy flowed freely that day

His Presence

In His presence is fullness of joy
So I gladly enter His presence
I know that I am welcome there
Jesus Christ made that clear
As He said, "It is finished"
Future's fear was vanquished
Loving Him, living for Him my Lord
Heaven forever is my reward
And I gladly enter His presence
So I gladly enter His presence

Jesus sits at God's right hand
Where pleasures are forevermore
I enter in gladly as I adore
His blessed appearance
Being changed into His image
He's won my deliverance
Loving Him, living for Him my Lord
Heaven forever is my reward
And I gladly enter His presence
So I gladly enter His presence

I Am One Year Older Today

I am one year older today
Seems like only yesterday
God's brought me a mighty long way
I'm so thankful I give Him praise
For all that He's done in my life
For victory, deliverance from strife
For answering prayers, providing my needs
His blessed assurance from sin, I'm set free
For loving me, leading me so tenderly
From coast to coast, from mountain to sea
My wonderful Shepherd is still leading me
So I shout, "Hallelujah" for all that He's done
My wonderful family, spectacular son
He saw fit to take home my daughter so dear
As I told her, we are coming soon, the time's drawing near
Until that day when our work here is done
Then we'll rise in the rays of the setting sun

Jesus Cares

Does Jesus care, really care?
Am I precious in His eyes?
Does He really collect my teardrops
In His bottle when I cry?

Does He feel my pain and heartache?
Is He listening when I pray?
Does He need to be reminded
Of my presence any day?

In His word, we have assurance
God is not a man, can't lie
God has promised to deliver
All His children He won't deny

His eyes roam along earth's pathways
Seeking saving all the lost
He loves all of His creation
Jesus died, none should be lost

If God gave His son up freely
To die a cruel death for our sins
Can we question such love poured out?
We are all precious to Him

Legacy of Love

Precious words Mom said to me
Live in love and unity
Give your heart to Jesus Christ
Let Him lead and guide your life
Read your Bible pray each day
Trust in Jesus all the way
Live in love and unity
That is love's sweet legacy

She loved the Lord
Believed His word
Prayed each and every day
His peace and joy were her delight
His love was her mainstay
Her children rose and called her blessed
Her life fulfilled a great success
Love's sweet, sweet legacy

That's love, sweet legacy
Sweet legacy of love
Live in love and unity
Enjoy love's sweet legacy
Love's sweet, sweet legacy

Life's Highway

Don't let failure be your master
Don't stay down whenever you fall
Let that moment be your teacher
A lesson to be learned that's all

Rise up quickly, brush the dust off
Intimidation doesn't mean defeat
Don't listen to the enemy's laughter
You were destined to be free

Free to walk unchained life's highway
Free to live, love, and succeed
Jesus Christ, the Heavenly Potentate
Of royal blood you are indeed

Stand upright straighten the weak knees
Lift your head up to the sky
God desires complete obedience
You are His child in Him abide

Failure's temporary, learn from mistakes
A baby trying to walk falls down
Watch him rise and try again
Soon he's walking round and round

Just remember God's sweet assurance
He'll be with you to the end
He's your Father, Christ your brother
The Holy Spirit your best friend

Winner take all, you are destined
To be victorious, to take the lead
So step focused on life's highway
To reach your goal, to win, succeed

Listen, Hear His Voice

I searched for true meaning
The meaning of life
I cried out to God
My voice raised to the sky
Father in heaven, if you're really real
Speak to me, help me, understand how I feel
Thunder high from heaven
Lightning flashes bolts divine
Let me see you, Mystic warrior
Show your power, let it fly

I ranted, raved, demanded, cried out
Hoping for a word, a thought, a sound
But my pleas for life's true meaning
Fell like arrows to the ground
When I felt time's passing unheard
When I knew the day was done
I had no answer, no divine assurance
Life's true meaning was still unfound

I felt defeated but could not give up
The search for true meaning, no answer, no change
I needed to know that in this vast cosmos
Someone was listening and heard my prayer
I then felt the silence, a calm sweet solitude
I stopped shouting and listened to my inner muse
The Holy Spirit then whispered in accents so low
My heart answered, "Dear God, thank
you, you speak to my soul."

Love Song

Sweet dreams of love in His arms
He keeps me safe from all harm
He cares, on His name I will call
He's my rock of defense, He's my all

Sweet dreams, in His love, I abide
I sleep sweetly, held by His side
I keep praising His holy name
Today, every day, He's the same

My name is beloved on His lips
He breathes, from His word, I will sip
My hearts filled with joy so divine
I'm my Savior's, and He is mine

Love's Mystery

The joys of living
In harmony and peace
The strength you give me
The comfort that I need
Your strong living hope
The dawn of each new day
The touch of my heart strings
Your delightful way
There's no end to your mystery
I still can't understand
The way you make me feel
At the touch of your hands

The Comforter indwells me
Confirms I'm saved by grace
The Spirit's mystery presence
Through me fully displayed
The sun's blazing beauty
The moon's gentle glow
The stars' merry twinkle
They all let me know
Creation joins the celebration
It's plain for all to see
That the mighty God of heaven
Really truly loves me

Mesmerized

Mesmerized by your glory
Mesmerized by your grace
Mesmerized by your mercy
When you took my place
Mesmerized by your coming
To our sinful earth
Mesmerized by your dying
Upon the cruel cross

God, I give you my life
God, I give you my all
God, I give you my moments
Upon you will I call

Your glory divine
On this heart of mine
Your grace poured out
On my soul, there's no doubt
Your mercy never ends
A new life begins
I'm mesmerized
That you did it all

Mind Control

Dear God, I ask you humbly
To soothe my mind, to banish fears
So many thoughts kept distant
In the past now reappear
They push their way into the present
Circling round and round in glee
Demanding I relinquish control
Trying to rewrite my destiny

Dear God, I know you know me
Know my weaknesses, my shame
I confess the truth, the promise
I'm delivered in your name
Holy Spirit, help and guide me
Lead me in paths of joy and peace
Stir the hope that at times lies dormant
You control my destiny

Dear God, I now take captive
Guard my mind, my thoughts control
The enemy's whisper is as poison
Trying to corrupt my very soul
Place a shield around your servant
Keep me sheltered from the storm
When at times I feel I'm sinking
I walk on water when you say, "Come."

Dear God, I give each moment
Every day into your care
God, I have your sweet assurance
Your presence will banish fear
You made me Father in Your image
That I'm Yours can't be denied
So take control of my heart and soul
My mind's at peace, on You relied

Never Alone

Sometimes I sit and ponder
Reflect on days now past and gone
Time goes by the moments fleeting
The cradle robber seems to have won
But I have the sweet conviction
Deep inside this heart of mine
That the God who gave me this life
Is the controller of life and time
When I feel as though forsaken
When I think I'm left alone
When I look around debating
He reminds I'm not alone

Never alone, His promise stands true
Time and tide are in His hands
Never alone by faith believing
Time and tide, heed His commands

The way is long, the road is narrow
I may feel at times dismay
But I hold on to His promise
He is with me all the way
Nothing comes that He can't control
Nothing takes Him by surprise
Nothing comes and overtakes me
Overlooked by watchful eyes
He never slumbers, sleeps, grows weary
My life, my times, are in His hands
I'm never alone His word reminds me
I'm never alone, His promise stands

No More Tears

He feels my pain
He sees my grief
Time and again
His comfort relieves
He knows my sorrow
He hears me call
He answers my heart
He soothes my soul

Jesus cried a long time ago
I feel He still cries
When He sees my woe
In time of leaving
The past behind
My Savior my Lord
Still weeps for mankind

I know it hurts
When a loved one goes
The distance between
It feeds your woe
Unable to touch
To hold them close
The Grim Reaper smiles
As he seeks for more

The day will come
When God says enough
My children have grieved

I've felt their loss
Time now begone
Your days they're done
Come home my child
The battle's won

No more tears
Let's wipe them away
Enjoy your life
In eternal day
Bask in My love
My glory divine
Will rest forever
On these that are mine

Our Wonderful Savior

Our wonderful Savior
Redeemer and Friend
His love has no boundaries
No distance no end
His love paid the price
The supreme sacrifice
We'll praise Him again and again

Forever and ever
His praises we'll sing
Giving glory and honor
To Jesus our King
We'll dance and adore Him
His name we'll lift high
He's the ruler of everything

His glory and grace
Deserving of praise
The joy He bestows
Reflects in every face
So filled to the brim
As we celebrate Him
Christ Jesus our Savior and Friend

Pains of the Past

Dear God, I come to you
Help me to make it through
Forgetting the pains of the past
They still seem to linger and last
Dear God, I come to you
Help me to make it through

My heart needs your healing touch
You know I love you so much
Dear God, deliver me
Dear God, please set me free
From memories filled with pain
Help me to face another day

Thank you, Father, you heard my cry
You touched my heart
You soothed my pain
You were always beside me in life
Always near, never far away

To you, I give my life
On you, I place my care
You've given me songs in the night
Courage to remember smile
And face each new day

Praises to Christ our King

The music is playing
The drumbeats are clear
I am highly expecting
As I draw near
My body is swaying
From side to side
I raise my hands high
I float on the tide
As I look around
Stamp my feet on the ground
As I worship my Savior and King
As I worship, His praises I sing

Let's worship and sing
Praise our Savior and King
He's worthy to be praised
Each moment we live
Each day we will give
All praises to Christ our King

Then without a sound
As praises ring out
The Holy Spirit attends
A sweet gentle breeze
We fall to our knees
As tear-filled eyes can be seen
God's presence is real
His Spirit is here

A holy hush surrounds
Fills the atmosphere
True worship to our Savior begins
All praises to Christ our King

So Happy
(Psalm 144)

The Lord is more than everything to me
Everything I need, He provides
I'm on His mind more than I can think
More than the sand on the seaside

The Lord is my strength, I sing a new song
Praises of joy I will sing
My deliverer, my teacher in Him, I will trust
My high tower, my fortress, my King

My sons, as plants, planted firm and deep
Trusting daily in His every word
My daughters as cornerstones, shining and sweet
Polished like a Palace all aglow

So happy am I that God is my Lord
So happy He's on my side
So happy to know that wherever I go
In God's love, I will abide

So Much to Be Thankful For

Each breath I take
Each precious new day
The vision to see things
Both near and far away
The mountains majestic
Their silver white peaks
The valleys and hills
Seem to beckon me
The green grassy meadows
The flower-filled fields
Their sweet perfume wafted
On the warm gentle breeze

The blue skies, the sunrise
The birds sing their tune
The sunlight revealing
The faint far distant moon
The bold rays of the bright sun
Staking claim to the day
Begone, moon, it's my turn
To shine forth my way
I smile as I whisper to God up above
Dear God, I am so thankful
You show me your love

Stand Still, Shine Forth

The Avenger is here
Our hearts beat fast
With the beginnings of fear
Dread till the fury's past
The Spirit within
He speaks soft and low
God's still in charge, beloved
Stand still, shine forth

Stand still in God's presence
The Most High's secret place
Stand still and abide
In His shadow of grace
Fear not, sing His praises
He remains in control
Shine forth in His glory
Stand still, shine forth

That's My God

That's my God
He looks out for me
That's my God
He set me free
My heart rejoices
In Him, I'm pleased
I'm filled with joy
My God and me

That's my God
My Father, it's true
That's my God
All I can do
Is praise His name
Shout hallelujahs to Him
How can it be
He died for me?

That's my God
My heart, it sings
That's my God
On joyful wings
Of song and love
Sent from above
That's my God
His name is love
That's my God
I have no fear
That's my God

Forever near
He lives in me
I live in Him
My life is His
Each day I live

The Book of Life

In the Lamb's book of life
My name's written down
I'll wear a robe of righteousness and crown
Play a harp sing His praise
Hallelujahs to raise
For my name's written down
Reserved a robe and a crown

On that hill far away
My Redeemer and friend
Gave His life on the cross
Satan's hold had to end
Jesus suffered and died
Willingly took my place
Now the Lamb's book of life
Has a line with my name

Oh, my friend, don't you see?
Perfect love rescued me
Just believe and receive
Jesus's blood brought victory
Over sin, death, and shame
On the cross took the blame
So our names can be found
In the book written down

The Good Old Days

The Bible's filled with stories
Of days so very long ago
The Patriarchs and the Pharaohs
Times of wisdom war and woe

Times of failures, times of triumphs
Nothing hidden all revealed
Good times, bad times all remembered
Those who died, others were healed

Tales of mankind's foolish follies
Trying to do things his own way
When instead like precious children
Heed the Father, stop the play

Life's no game, there is great danger
Of falling helpless in the pit
Then be sold to a new Master
Satan's stronghold, the belly of a fish

God the Father rich in mercy
Waits on prodigals to come home
Welcomes them, then throws a party
Forgiving sins and all they'd done

Nothing escapes His eyes of vigilance
Roaming the earth both far and wide
Seeking, saving, loving, leading
Hapless weary ones their guide

The Heavenly Host

Be the stars
Twinkle, twinkle, let your lights shine
In the darkness of this world
Reflect His glory His joy divine
To men, women, boys, and girls
Show forth His love to everyone
In His image, He made us all
In His likeness, we're fashioned
Created by love
To be lovers of everyone

Be the sun
Shine forth, spread your glorious warmth
The world is cold each living soul
Needs heat and love to survive
Glow brightly shine forth
The Redeemer lives on
The fight is won
He's redeemed the world
Each man woman boy and girl

Be the moon
Glow brightly, shine forth in the darkness and gloom
He delivered mankind from death
To the ones who accept Him, believing His word
He's erased the long list of sin's debt

Twinkle, shine, and glow
Mankind's delivered from woe
Accept this free gift of His love
He died for all
Each man, woman, boy, and girl
Heavenly host, go show forth God's love

The Mighty Seed
(Psalms 112:1-3)

I fear the Lord
In Him, I am blessed
I have great delight
In His commandments
God promised my seed
Will truly be blessed
Live in righteousness
Mighty on earth

Mighty on earth
My seed is blessed
Riches and wealth
God's promises
Forever endure
Blessings secure
The mighty seed
Live in righteousness

I stand upright
Generations are blessed
Blessed of the Lord
In His righteousness
They greatly delight
In His commandments
God promised their seed
Will be mighty on earth

Mighty on earth
Their seed is blessed
Riches and wealth
God's promises
Forever endure
Blessings secure
The mighty seed
Live in righteousness

The Wedding

God's intentions are honorable
He has a wedding in mind
He's selected the Bridegroom
The lover of all mankind

Jesus Christ loves completely
Satisfaction guaranteed
You're no longer sin's captive
He's all that you need

God the Father, Giver Almighty
God the Son, tried and true
God the Holy Spirit the witness
And the Bride says, "I do."

The Word of God
(Psalm 119)

The word of God is true, a treasure trove
Better than thousands of silver and gold
I delight in its riches, its wealth untold
I rejoice as if I've found great spoil

I think on the word, I comfort myself
My sufferings aren't worthy to compare
With the glory revealed, the love I share
The word is pure, will forever endure

I hide the word way down deep in my heart
From sin, I will cleanse my way
To the word I will heed, meditate night and day
Great peace floods my soul as the word I obey

Thy word is a shining lamp to my feet
A light to the path where I went
It accomplishes and prospers by God it was sent
Sweeter than honey are the words to my taste

Three in One

I want to please my God and father
Jesus Christ, His only begotten son
And the precious Holy Spirit
The wonderful three in one
Sometimes I feel a little weary
Unsure of if I've done right or wrong
I realize that the only answer
Is the wonderful three in one

Remind me that you love me
Fill my heart with joy and peace
I need your sweet assurance
Your kind comfort and release

I know the devil's busy
Trying to steal my joy and peace
There's one thing I know is settled
Is my delight, my hope in three

Yes you're pleased with me, my Father
The question settled by Christ the Son
Holy Spirit, take me deeper
In the love of the three in one

To Tell You the Truth

My life so complicated
My thoughts far and wide
Adrift on life's highway
A piece of flotsam on the tide

Life's dealt me its blows
Calculated to kill
All my hopes and ambitions
My sweet dreams and my will

"But not so," said the Father
You've remained on my mind
The truth is beloved
You're blessed by the divine

Shaped for visions of rapture
Sweet destiny's own child
Your deliverance determined
Tho' Satan beguiled

Jesus Christ, your Redeemer
Gave His life on the cross
Bought your eternal redemption
The truth is Saved, not lost

Unseen Angels

When I'm faced with fear
And strong feelings of dread
Come over my soul
Thoughts of doom filling my head

The shadows hang low
Filled with monsters that grow
Into fiends, all around
I'm dry of mouth with no sound

Then piercing the gloom
Dispatched quickly my way
Unseen angels surround me
Guardians of grace

Ministering spirits sent forth
They banish all fear
They strengthen and deliver
God's children so dear

We're never alone
Without help sent our way
God sits on His throne
Angel armies prepared

We Can Trust Him

We hear the news, see daily newscasts
Every day brings words of woe
Mankind's lost, there's no deliverance
The powers that be barely offer hope

Stores are closing, churches shuttered
No glimpse of light, is there no end?
Can't we combat this deadly enemy
Work together, the world a friend?

Things are getting worse, more problems
We seek answers without, within
Reminds us of Sodom, Gomorrah
God destroyed all because of sin

Yet among the unbelievers
Lived a man named Lot, we're told
Though he had his dwelling among them
His life was spent in God's sacred mold

His soul was vexed to see their conduct
Refusing to heed God's laws or ways
They had no time, they loved their pleasures
Who cared about God, the Ancient of Days?

It's now we live for, grab the good life
Fully steaming on ahead
None can stop us, none can hinder
What we do, we'll make our bed

Till the time God's wrath was poured out
Lot and family were spared
Mrs. Lot failed to heed the warning
A pillar of salt she was soon displayed

Let's heed the lesson, turn to Jesus
Repent, pray, God's face let us seek
He's a God who keeps His promise
To deliver the weary, worn and weak

Win the War, Win the Fight

From morning till night
From dawn till daylight
Fix your mind on Jesus Christ
Win the war, win the fight
Thoughts are wild and go astray
Reliving each moment of pain
I'm a failure to yourself, you say
How can I face another day?
Fix your mind on Jesus Christ
Win the war, win the fight

So don't focus on things you've done
Remember Christ's victory, the battle won
His righteousness He exchanged for your sin
You opened your heart and let Him in
You received precious promises life anew
Freedom to live worship in all you do
Jesus Christ is your Savior, on Him now depend
You've a heavenly Father, your life has no end
Eternally yours is how you sign your name
Born again by the Spirit, no longer enslaved
Fix your mind on Jesus Christ
You've won the war, you've won the fight

Worship the Lord in Spirit and Truth

The Father seeketh such
He loves you so much
Give Him your heart, your tongue, your praise
Give Him your voice
Sweet fragrances, your choice
Each note now joyfully raise

Come praise your God, your Savior, your King
He's deserving of everything
He's the ruler of the universe
All creation is subject to Him
Let true worship now begin
In His love, your being immerse

Lift your hands and voices to sing
Saturate your soul in song and hymn
Hallelujahs now rejoice
Shout aloud, leap for joy
In spirit and truth, let's worship the Lord
Let's worship the Lord according to His word
In spirit and truth, let's worship the Lord
In spirit and truth, let's worship the Lord

You Chose Me

What did you see in me?
What made you call my name?
So homely, I did agree
But you took away all my shame

You chose me, you chose me
It's a wonder that you chose me
My heart was amazed
A new song I sing
The King of all Kings
Did choose me

You lifted me up on high
Clothed me in your righteousness
Beyond forever, eternity's time
Disappears in God's holy light

Part 2

Be Strong

Be strong, little children
Be strong in the Lord
Be strong, little children
Be strong in the Lord

Clap your hands, stamp your feet
Dance around, hear the beat
Be strong, little children
Be strong in the Lord
Be strong, little children
Be strong in the Lord

Don't Be Scared

Don't be scared

Don't be scared

Jesus loves you

Don't be afraid

He knows where you are

He knows and He cares

Jesus loves you

Don't be scared

Jesus loves you

Don't be scared

God Made Me

God made man in His image
That includes me
He made me to love
He made me to hope
He made me to live and be free

God so loved the world
That includes me
He made me to love Him first, then the rest
He made me to hope for the best
He made me to live and be free in Him
He made me to be blessed
He made me to be blessed

God Never Stops Loving Me

God loves me today
God loved me yesterday
God will love me tomorrow
God loves me every day

God never stops loving me
God never stops loving me
He loves me from my head to my feet
God never stops loving me

I will love Him today
More than yesterday
I will love Him tomorrow
I will love Him every day

I will never stop loving Him
I will never stop loving Him
He loves me from my head to my feet
God never stops loving me
God never stops loving me

Heaven

Heaven is a beautiful place
God lives there, God lives there
Jesus said we'll all go someday
To heaven, that beautiful, beautiful place

We'll sing and shout and dance for joy
In heaven, that beautiful, beautiful place
We'll see the Angels, girls and boys
In heaven, that beautiful, beautiful place

Hooray for Jesus

I love to dance around
I love to sing and play
When my feet hit the ground
I shout "Hooray, hooray for Jesus!"

I love to kneel and pray
I love to sing and play
When my feet hit the ground
I shout, "Hooray, hooray for Jesus!"

I read my Bible every day
I love to sing and play
When my feet hit the ground
I shout, "Hooray, hooray for Jesus!"

I Can Count

One, Two
I love Jesus, I do: I love Jesus I do
Three, Four
I opened my heart's door: I opened my heart's door
Five, Six
That's all it takes: That's all it takes
Seven, Eight
It's not too late: It's not too late
Nine, Ten
Let Jesus come in: Let Jesus come in

I Don't Want the Stones to Cry Out

I love to praise God
With all of my might
I love to worship God
Both day and night
I don't want the stones to cry out, cry out
I don't want the stones to cry out, cry out

So I'll worship and praise
My voice I will raise
I'll sing and I'll shout
I'll dance all about
I don't want the stones to cry out, cry out
I don't want the stones to cry out, cry out

I Love to Read the Bible

I love to read the Bible
It is God's word that says
How God our Father in heaven
Sent Jesus to earth one day

Jesus was born a baby
To the stables the shepherds came
After the angels were singing
And told them where He lay

The shepherds came first to see Jesus
Then wise men came from afar
Bringing many gifts on their camels
Following a bright new star

Jesus became man, then our Savior
He died on the cross for our sins
He rose from the grave, went back to heaven
Making a way for us to go in

So we children can come to Jesus
Bringing gifts of love from our hearts
He loves us so, His word we know
From His children, He'll never depart

Jesus Is the Light

Who loves the dark? Not me
In the dark, I'm not able to see
I just stumble around
With my feet on the ground
In the dark, I'm not able to see

I wake in the morning light
Ready to start a new day
I don't stumble around
With my feet on the ground
In the light, I can see my way

I want to see my way
In the light, I can see my way
Jesus is the light of the world
In Him, I can see my way
I don't stumble around
With my feet on the ground
In Jesus, I can see my way

Jesus, the Miracle Worker

Jesus did many miracles
When He was on earth long ago
He turned water into wine at the wedding
He opened blind eyes made them see
He fed many people, when food they were needing
He walked on water, calmed the stormy sea
He healed the sick and the lame
He made the deaf hear again
He raised people from the dead, gave them life
He taught us to live in love, not strife
A miracle worker was He
Oh, how He loves you and me
His miracles prove, His love we can't lose
Oh, how He loves you and me
The miracle worker loves me

Nothing, Absolutely Nothing

Nothing, absolutely nothing
Compares to the love of the Lord
Nothing, absolutely nothing
Compares to the love of the Lord
Joy He brings
Songs we sing
Blessings we share
His love's everywhere
Nothing, absolutely nothing
Compares to the love of the Lord
Nothing, absolutely nothing
Compares to the love of the Lord

Pitter-Patter Goes the Rain

Pitter-patter goes the rain
Falling on my windowpane
While in bed, I'm tucked in tight
I love it when it falls at night

In the morning, when I wake
I give God thanks for a new day
For all the flowers that are in bloom
Mom cut some daisies for her room

God gives the rain for plants to grow
The sun to shine, the wind that blows
For boys and girls to run and play
We thank you God for each new day

Sing and Cry Out

Sing a hymn
Sing a song
Sing to Jesus
All the day long
For God is great
He's worthy of praise
Sing unto Him and cry out

Shout aloud
Let your voice be heard
Hallelujahs
As God deserves
If we don't praise
The name of the Lord
We'll battle the rocks
They'll cry out

The heavens declare
The glory of God
The skies show forth
His handiwork
Day by day, their voices are heard
The darkness of night
Shows He's Lord

So Special

Today is a very special day
You opened your eyes
You were in for a big surprise
Here comes a wish
Filled with God's love
Sent to you from heaven above

You're so special, so special
Just as you've always been
He loves you so much
He's as close as your need
Open your eyes to this big surprise
Sent to you with love from heaven above

God loves you, He loves you
More than you'll ever know
Here comes a wish
Filled with God's love
Receive it now from heaven above
Open your eyes to a big surprise

Someone Special

Come, little children, gather around
Listen to a story that's true
A long time ago
Before you were born
God wanted a little boy and a little girl
To join a family He knew
Who was that little boy?
Who was that little girl?
Someone that God knew
A special someone
That's you

You're special, so special
That's me, that's you
You're someone special God knew
God wanted a little boy
God wanted a little girl
To join a family He knew
That special someone was you
I'm that special someone God knew

That's How It Should Be

Little children live in love
Love and unity
Little children live in love
That's how it should be

Little children praise His name
Like birds on a tree
Little children praise His name
That's how it should be

Little children now rejoice
Shout as loud as could be
Little children now rejoice
That's how it should be

Little children trust in God
He loves you and me
Little children trust in God
That's how it should be

That's Why Jesus Died

Jesus died upon the cross
Why did Jesus die?
He died for my sins and yours
That's why Jesus died

Heaven is a holy place
No sin can enter there
Jesus took our sins away
That's why Jesus died

Jesus rose and went to heaven
To prepare for us a place
We'll rise, just like He's leaving
To live in heaven, that beautiful place

The Bible Tells

The Bible tells us of God's love
How Jesus came to earth
It tells of Angels, shepherds
Of Jesus's special birth
It tells of wise men traveling far
The gifts that they did bring
Gold, frankincense, and myrrh
That was their offering

The Bible tells of people's lives
The good times and the bad
It tells us if you trust in God
The blessings you will have
It tells how Jesus gave His life
Upon that cruel cross
The disciples saw the empty tomb
They thought that all was lost

The Bible tells us of God's plan
To take us to heaven one day
That's why Jesus rose, went back home
To heaven so far away
He's building beautiful mansions
For us who on Him believe
He loved us first, let's love Him back
And eternal life receive

The Dog Fight

Dogs in the neighborhood far and near
Come running to the Doggie Fair
Clothed some in black and white
Just look at them, they're a pretty sight

Soon coming from one neighbor's grounds
Are heard a lot of angry sounds
The dogs' tails stiffen, for they know, you see
That new dog's coming, some wait fearfully

Now the new dog just moved in, he's a bulldog
He's so strong, he can pull a log
The dogs dare not fight him, for they know
That he's a champion dog
See, he wears a blue bow

The games soon start, all are having fun
The new dog starts to fight the old Greyhound
The dogs stop playing and gather around
When suddenly, the old Greyhound charges
That new dog, the bully's thrown to the ground

The dogs start cheering, the bully's unable to rise
The old greyhound's newfound glory reaches the skies
Disgraced, humiliated, the bulldog slinks away
Vowing revenge on the old Greyhound some other day

The lesson learned by all the dogs at play
Is to treat others kindly, listen to what they have to say
Don't be a bully, fussing and fighting with all you meet
So much better to live in love and unity

Turkey for Timmy

"Oh, Mommy, not turkey again,"
Little Timmy pouted and cried.
"We've had that for so many days
I'm sick of it," he sighed.

"I won't cook it tomorrow, dear,"
His mother consoled him.
"Try to eat as much as you can
Don't waste food, now begin."

Timmy ate half of his turkey stew
Then said he could eat no more
He left the table washed his hands
Then bounded through the door

The doorbell rang very loudly
Timmy's mom got up with a frown
"I wonder who that can be," she said.
It was their friend old, Mr. Brown

"Your husband sent me to tell you
That he has lost his job
He'll be coming back this afternoon."
Timmy's mother began to sob

The back door opened quietly
Little Timmy came inside
When he saw his mother crying
His brown eyes opened wide

"Son, the turkey you despise so much
You won't get even that now."
She explained to him more in detail
When he began to knit his brow

Now Timmy doesn't grumble about what he eats
He gives thanks to God with a smile
He remembers the turkey he never did like
He's had nothing so special in a while

CPSIA information can be obtained
at www.ICGtesting.com
Printed in the USA
BVHW091021171120
593515BV00017B/1274

9 781647 733605